READING REINFORCERS FOR THE PRIMARY GRADES

by Imogene Forte

Incentive Publications, Inc.
Nashville, Tennessee

Illustrated by Gayle Seaberg Harvey
Cover by Geoffrey Brittingham
Edited by Leslie Britt

ISBN 0-86530-278-2

PRINTED IN THE UNITED STATES OF AMERICA

Table of Contents

Preface 7

Seek and Find Vowel Sounds *(Using Vowel Sounds)*.................................9

Word Makeover *(Using Initial Consonants)* 10

The Great Consonant Case *(Recognizing and Using Consonants)* 11

Silent Skyscraper *(Recognizing Silent Consonants)*.............................12

Is It "D" or "T"? *(Recognizing Word Endings)* 14

Letter-ing *(Recognizing Word Endings)* 15

Look-Alikes *(Final Sound Discrimination/Word Association)* 16

Wordly Wise *(Combining Beginning and Ending Sounds to Make Words)* 18

Under the Phonics Umbrella *(Recognizing Consonants and Vowels)*...............20

Phonics Foolers *(Using Phonetic Symbols)* 21

Circle Around *(Using Rhyming Words)* 22

Super Shape-Up *(Recognizing and Using Rhyming Words)* 23

Syllable Sail *(Identifying and Using Syllables)*..............................28

Speaking in Syllables *(Recognizing and Using Syllables)* 30

The Big Mark-Up *(Using Accent Marks)*...32

Extend-a-Word *(Adding Endings to Root Words)* 33

Prefix Pinup *(Using Prefixes)*..34

Word Slide *(Recognizing and Using Compound Words)*............................36

Compound Canvas *(Recognizing and Using Compound Words)*.......................37

Compound Countdown *(Recognizing and Using Compound Words)*....................38

Compound Museum *(Recognizing and Using Compound Words)* 39

Word Clouds *(Distinguishing Between Words That Look Similar)*..................40

Vocabulary Vault *(Using Sight Word Vocabulary)* 41

Add-a-Word *(Using Sight Word Vocabulary)*.....................................42

Rebus Race *(Using Picture Clues)* 43

Rebus Race II *(Using Picture Clues)* 44

In Context *(Using Context Clues)* 45

Grammar Cracker Cake *(Defining Words by Classification or Function)* 47

Classification Jumble *(Defining Words by Classification or Function)* 48

On the Flip Side *(Understanding Multiple Meanings)*...........................49

Pair Up (*Using Homonyms*) 50

The Leaning Tower of Pairs
 (*Using Synonyms, Antonyms, and Homonyms*) 52

Vocabulary Variety (*Using Content-Area Vocabulary*) 54

Greetings (*Associating Words with Feelings*) 55

An Orange Is an Orange (*Forming Sensory Impressions*) 56

Sensational Sentences
 (*Interpreting and Conveying Moods Created by Words*) 57

Hue Me In! (*Interpreting and Conveying Moods Created by Words*) 59

Holiday Check-Up (*Recognizing Word Relationships*) 60

On the Word Track (*Recognizing Word Relationships*) 61

Construction Crew (*Developing Word Appreciation*) 63

Word of the Day (*Word Appreciation*) 64

Vacation Village (*Vocabulary Development*) 65

Topic Centered (*Categorization/Word Association*) 66

Apple Treats (*Word Association*) 67

Cinderella's Closet (*Classification*) 68

Logical Line-Up (*Listing Ideas in Proper Sequence*) 69

Sequence of Events (*Sequencing*) 70

Think Tank (*Drawing Conclusions*) 71

Concluding Conclusions (*Drawing Conclusions*) 73

Just Because (*Determining Cause and Effect*) 74

With Pen in Hand (*Sensitivity to Author's Purpose*) 75

Plot a Characterization (*Identifying Character Traits*) 76

Finger Talk (*Recognizing and Using Character Traits*) 78

Stories To Build (*Sensitivity to Plot and Sequence*) 80

Cartoon Creations (*Visualizing*) 82

Lettered Lunches (*Alphabetizing*) 83

Oops! Wrong Page! (*Using the Dictionary*) 85

Contemplating the Contents (*Using a Table of Contents*) 86

A Plain Paper Plane Plan (*Reading and Following Picture Directions*) 88

Punctuation Pointers (*Recognizing Punctuation Marks*) 89

Little Books Tell a Lot (*Reading and Following Written Directions*) 90

Fruit Salad (*Reading and Following Written Directions*) 92

Answer Keys 93

Preface

Reading Reinforcers for the Primary Grades provides a series of reading skills-sequenced activities planned to reinforce and supplement the literature-based whole language curriculum. The importance of skills-based supplementary activities in promoting reading independence cannot be overemphasized. The activities may be used for total group instruction, with small groups, or selectively to meet individual student needs. They have been carefully designed to promote the skills needed for successful independent reading. Among these skills are:

- sound discrimination
- word association
- recognizing and understanding syllables
- recognizing and understanding compound words
- word classification
- using synonyms, antonyms, and homonyms
- developing word appreciation
- sequencing ideas
- understanding author's intent

The material in *Reading Reinforcers* has been divided into teacher pages and student activity pages. A teacher page presents an activity's Purpose (the skill being promoted), Preparation (materials needed, preparatory instructions, and special considerations), and Procedure (the activity's rules or instructions, often intended to be rewritten or summarized for student use). Student activity pages may be reproduced for classroom use or may be copied on a chart or chalkboard. These activities are presented in a wide variety of formats ranging from teacher-directed interactive lessons, games and game boards, word-find and crossword puzzles, and cooperative learning projects to independent student worksheets. For convenience, student pages have been designed as single-page activities.

In order to be easily identifiable, activities are sequentially grouped in basic skills areas. Skills are listed after activity titles in the table of contents, as well as on each teacher and student activity page. While the skills promoted in the activities increase in difficulty, it is not necessary that they be used in the order in which they are presented—each activity may be used individually and independently of any other.

The activities in this book are designed to increase children's ability to read with greater accuracy, comprehension, and fluency and to contribute to a firm foundation for a lifelong love of reading.

✣ SEEK AND FIND VOWEL SOUNDS ✣

PURPOSE: Using vowel sounds

PREPARATION

1. Gather the following materials:
   - 3″ x 5″ index cards
   - pencils
   - magazines
   - scissors

2. Cut from magazines (or draw) pictures of objects easily found in the classroom or on the playground. Glue these pictures on index cards.

3. Provide extra blank index cards and pencils.

   Note: This is not a game to play with the whole class or with a large group of students. It is ideal for small reading groups or for two or three children who need extra reinforcement. Most groups will need about ten minutes to complete the activity.

PROCEDURE

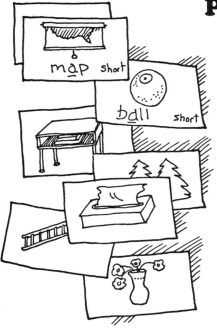

1. Select four or five cards from the stack, and try to locate the objects in the assigned time period.

2. As each object is located, write its name on the index card provided. Underline the vowel sound, and next to the word tell if it is a long or a short vowel.

3. Continue until all objects are located and recorded.

4. The student who finishes first or who locates the most objects within the allotted amount of time wins the game.

✦ WORD MAKEOVER ✦

PURPOSE: Using initial consonants

PREPARATION

1. Use the patterns on this page to prepare tagboard word squares and consonant letter strips as shown in the illustration.

2. Provide pencils and paper for student use, and place all materials in a convenient spot for students to use as a free-time activity.

PROCEDURE

1. Choose a letter strip and a square.

2. Pull the strip through the opening in the square to make words by combining the initial consonants with the other letters.

3. Write your new words on a separate sheet of paper.

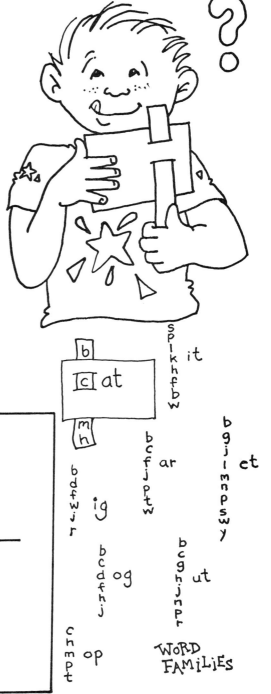

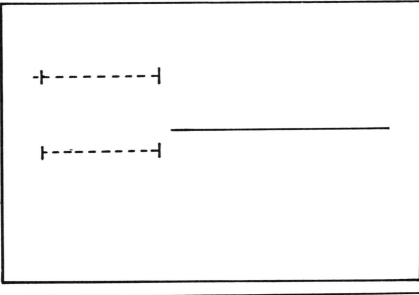

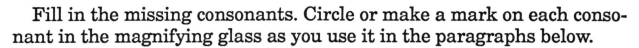

THE GREAT CONSONANT CASE

Fill in the missing consonants. Circle or make a mark on each consonant in the magnifying glass as you use it in the paragraphs below.

I__ you wor__ care__ully, you ca__ __ind the missin__ consonan__s ri__ht un__er Sly Sam t__e Sleut__'s eyes. Cir__le a co__sonant whe__ you __ut it in its p__oper pla__e, and you will __now __ot to go loo__ing __or it a__ain.

__ly Sa__ ha__ bee__ a__si__ne__ __o the __reat Co__sonan__ Ca__e. __on__onants __eep __isappea__ing i__ lar__e num__ers ri__ht ou__ o__ othe__wi__e sensi__le sen__ence__. More consonants a__e mis__ing eve__y __ay. The wor__s a__e be__inning to __anic, and thou__h Sly Sam i__ smar__ and __rave, eve__ he is desperate. Ca__ you co__e to his re__cue?

Please hu__ __y and repla__e the missing consonants to re__urn peace and __uiet to Sly Sam's worl__.

The one stray vowel and five leftover consonants create a message to you from Sly Sam. Write the message here: "_____!!"

Name _____ Date _____

✤ SILENT SKYSCRAPER ✤

PURPOSE: Recognizing silent consonants

PREPARATION

Provide a pencil and a copy of the Silent Skyscraper dot-to-dot puzzle on page 13 for each participant.

PROCEDURE

Begin at dot #1 and quietly pronounce the word. If the word contains a silent consonant, find the next word in numerical order with a silent consonant, and draw a line between the two. (If the very next word does not contain a silent consonant, skip that word and proceed to the next one.) Continue connecting the words with silent consonants until the drawing is completed.

SILENT SKYSCRAPER

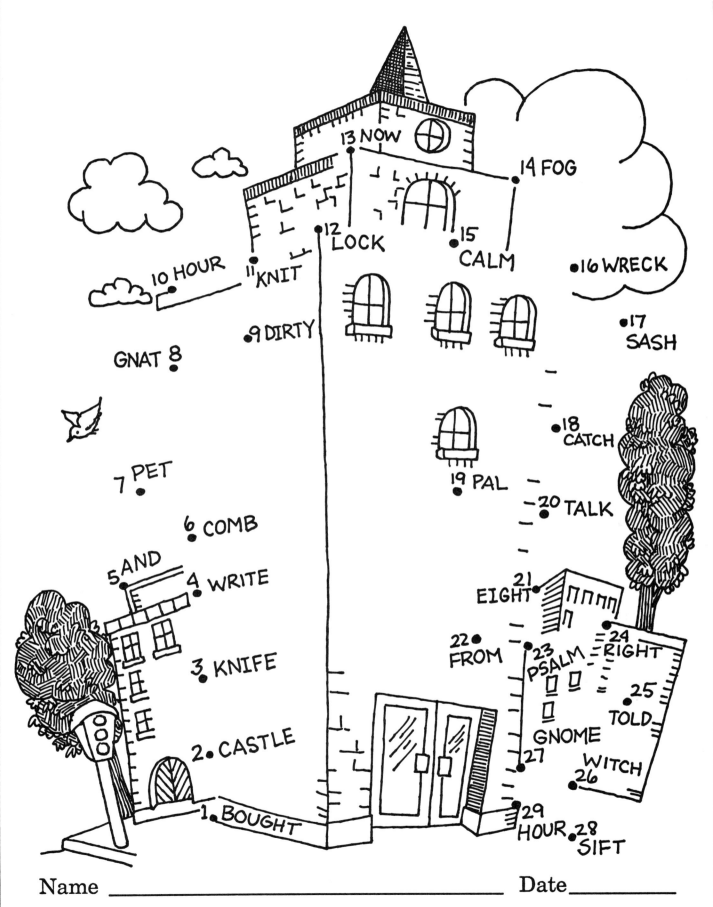

Name _____

Date _____

IS IT "D" OR "T"?

When **-ed** is added to the end of a word but does not form a separate syllable, the **-ed** will sound like either a **D** or a **T**. Read the words below, and write the words with **D** ending sounds in the large **D** shape below and the words with **T** ending sounds in the large **T** shape below.

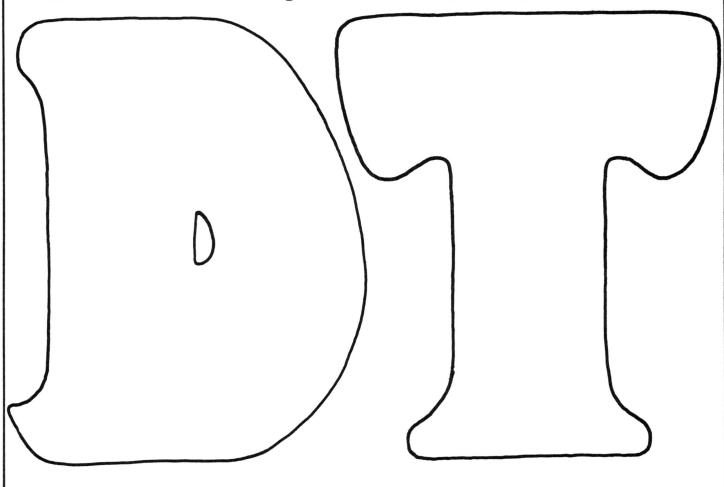

Looked	Called	Marched	Entered	Dumped
Smoked	Bumped	Slashed	Tamed	Added
Shocked	Stacked	Followed	Thrilled	Salted
Walked	Rolled	Bricked	Framed	Picked
Charged	Planted	Thanked	Filled	Jerked
Allowed	Tracked	Dreamed	Harmed	Tricked

Write five more words with **-ed** endings that sound like **T** and five more words with **-ed** endings that sound like **D**.

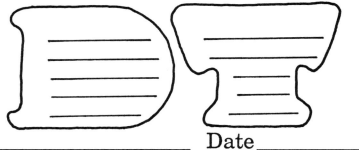

Name _____ Date _____

Read the words below and decide if the last letter in each word should be doubled or dropped before adding the -ing suffix. Write each new word ending with -ing in the correct letter boxes below.

hop	plan	time	sit	live	hope
come	wake	tap	swim	love	bat
grin	snore	strike	fan	trim	like

Name _____   Date_____

✤ LOOK-ALIKES ✤

PURPOSE: Final sound discrimination/word association

PREPARATION

Make copies of the Look-Alikes worksheet (page 17), and give one to each student.

PROCEDURE

A. Final Sound Discrimination

1. The teacher chooses one word from each block and reads it aloud.

2. Students listen as the teacher reads each word. The students then draw a circle around the word the teacher pronounced.

B. Word Association

1. Students cross out the word that does not belong.

2. Students then draw a star around the plural form of each word.

1.	PENCILS	PENNY	PENCIL
2.	PAN	PAT	PANS
3.	TOE	TOES	TOP
4.	HATS	HOT	HAT
5.	TREE	SEE	TREES
6.	STOP	STOPS	STRIP
7.	COW	COT	COWS
8.	BALL	BELLS	BELL
9.	BUG	BAG	BUGS
10.	ROCKS	RACK	ROCK
11.	STRAPS	STRIP	STRAP
12.	STRING	BRING	STRINGS

Name _____ Date _____

✤ WORDLY WISE ✤

PURPOSE: Combining beginning and ending sounds to make words

PREPARATION

1. Provide the following materials:
   - game board
   - 3" x 5" index cards
   - markers
   - spinner
   - pencils and paper for scorekeeping

2. Reproduce the Wordly Wise game board (page 19).

3. Write the ending sounds on cards.

4. Provide a marker for each player.

5. Place the game in a learning center or in a free-time activity center.

PROCEDURE

1. This game is for three or more players.

2. Place the cards face down on the game board.

3. The first player spins, moves that number of spaces, and draws a card. Using the ending sound on the card and the beginning sound in the square landed on, the player creates as many words as possible. Extra letters or syllables may be added in the middle as long as the beginning and ending sounds remain in place.

   Example: Beginning sound—bl   Ending sound—ed
   Words Formed:
   Bled
   Blinked
   Blurted
   Bloated

   A player's score for each turn equals the number of words made during that turn.

4. Players continue to take turns until one reaches twenty-five points and wins the game.

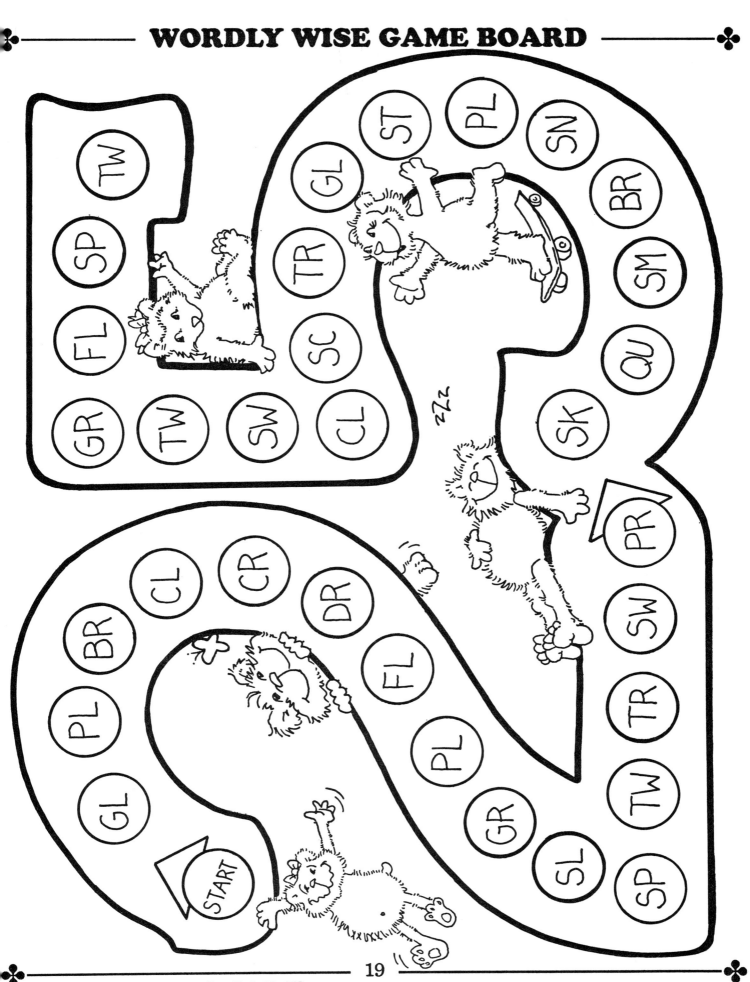

Color all of the consonant spaces in the umbrella yellow.
Color all of the vowel spaces orange.
Color the rest of the picture as you like.

Circle all of the long U sounds in the following sentence:

Ursula Upchurch usually waited under the umbrella until her uncle

unpacked his unused ukulele.

Name _____ Date _____

©1994 by Incentive Publications, Inc., Nashville, TN.

A Phonics Fooler is a joke or rhyme written in phonetic notation. Translate this fooler by writing its standard spelling version on the lines beside it.

Yōō dōn't nēd ā rōō'-lər   _____
Tōō trăns-lāt' thĭs fōō'-lər   _____
Jŭst yōōz ôl yōō nō   _____
ə-bout' fŏn'-ĭks, ənd GŌ!   _____

Make up 6 Phonetic Foolers of your own, and write them in the spaces below. (Find the correct phonetic form for each word in a dictionary.) Exchange papers with a classmate, and rewrite his or her Foolers in standard spelling. Then discuss your translations.

Name _____   Date _____

✤ CIRCLE AROUND ✤

PURPOSE: Using rhyming words

PREPARATION

1. Gather the following materials:
   - black or red construction paper
   - magazine pictures
   - scissors
   - tagboard
   - paste
   - container and top

2. Cut several small circles from the tagboard, and paste magazine pictures of various common objects on them.

3. Cut larger circles from black or red construction paper. Make a slit in each circle in order that tagboard circles can be inserted into them.

4. Place all of the materials in a decorated container, and print the game's title on the outside of the container.

PROCEDURE

1. Choose a tagboard circle from the container.

2. Insert it into the construction paper slit.

3. Name as many words as possible that rhyme with the picture.

hat
rat
mat
sat
pat

✤ SUPER SHAPE-UP ✤

PURPOSE: Recognizing and using rhyming words

PREPARATION

1. Glue the two halves of the Super Shape-Up game board (pages 24-25) inside a file folder.

2. Reproduce the Super Shape-Up rhyming word sheets (pages 26-27), and cut the shapes apart. Place them in an envelope.

3. On the outside of the envelope, print the directions given below.

4. Place the folder and the envelope in an accessible place for individual student use.

PROCEDURE

1. Match the rhyming pictures, and place them on the correct shapes.

2. Pronounce the words represented by each picture.

ADAPTATIONS

This game could be adapted to teach word association by using words in the squares, or to teach upper- and lower-case letter recognition by putting letters in the squares.

♣ SYLLABLE SAIL ♣

PURPOSE: Identifying and using syllables

PREPARATION

1. Enlarge the Syllable Sail game board (page 29).

2. Cut sailboat markers from construction paper.

3. Make word cards with the following or other ocean-related words:

Sailing	Aquanaut	Sponges	Underwater
Ocean	Coral	Algae	Depth
Vessel	Snorkel	Fathom	Stern
Waves	Plankton	Whale	Aqualung
Porpoise	Scuba	Ship	Lighthouse
Mollusks	Ahoy	Bow	Regatta
Port	Starboard	Boat	Swimmers
Divers	Deck	Sea	Oceanography

PROCEDURE

1. This game is for two or more players.

2. Place the stack of word cards in the center of the board.

3. Each player selects a sailboat marker and places it on the board.

4. Players take turns drawing a card and moving one space forward for each syllable in the word on the card. If the number of syllables is incorrectly guessed, the player moves back that same number of syllables.

5. The first player to reach Home Port wins the game.

✣ SPEAKING IN SYLLABLES ✣

PURPOSE: Recognizing and using syllables

PREPARATION

1. Provide the following materials for the students:
   - Speaking in Syllables game board (page 31)
   - Markers
   - Die

2. Reproduce the Speaking in Syllables game board. Write other one-, two-, and three-syllable words in the squares if the ones shown are not appropriate for your students' ability level.

3. Provide one die and a marker for each student.

PROCEDURE

1. This game is for two or more players.

2. The first player throws the die and moves the marker forward that number of spaces. If the square landed on contains a one-syllable word, the player pronounces the word correctly and moves forward one space. If the marker lands on a space containing a two-syllable word, the player pronounces the word and moves forward two spaces. If the player lands on a three-syllable word and pronounces the word correctly, he or she receives an extra turn. (If the player mispronounces the word, the extra turn is forfeited.) If players mispronounce their words, they must move their markers back the same number of spaces as the number of syllables in the words.

3. The other players continue the game in the same manner. The first player to go around the board three times wins the game.

SLOW DOWN!
INCHWORM CROSSING

FINISH

ACT
LIKE
BUNDLE
TENNIS
ROT
WINDY
FIFTY
PROPERTY
DIRECTOR
TIRESOME
TWINKLE
PANIC
BIT
PONY
TRUTH
CARROT
HAPPINESS
DANGEROUS
BACON
WHO
VISIT
ONE
STRUGGLE
GALLOP
BALLOON
EARLY
POTTERY
FULL
ACTION
START

✣ THE BIG MARK-UP ✣

PURPOSE: Using accent marks

PREPARATION

1. Using brightly colored felt-tipped pens, line sheets of writing paper to make three vertical columns. Provide one sheet for each student.

2. Print two- and three-syllable words on 3″ x 5″ cards or on strips of construction paper.

3. Place the words in a box or basket, and pass it around for each student to select twenty cards. (Adjust the number of the cards to the maturity level of the students.)

4. Provide the vertically-lined paper, scissors, paste, pencils, and the Procedure directions for the students.

PROCEDURE

1. Read each of your words carefully.

2. Cut each word apart into syllables.

3. Paste one syllable in each column.

4. Place accent marks in the correct places.

5. Write your full name on the bottom of the paper. Divide your name into syllables, and place the accent marks correctly.

✤ EXTEND-A-WORD ✤

PURPOSE: Adding endings to root words

PREPARATION

1. Gather the following materials:
   – 3″ x 5″ cards
   – felt-tipped pen
   – paper
   – pencils

2. Write root words on one set of 3″ x 5″ cards

3. Write word endings on a second set of 3″ x 5″ cards.

4. Place the two stacks of cards in a quiet corner along with writing paper and pencils for student use.

PROCEDURE

1. This activity is for individual student use.

2. Choose one root word card.

3. Find as many word endings as possible which can be added to that word to make new words.

4. Write the root word at the top of a sheet of paper, and beneath it list the new words you created.

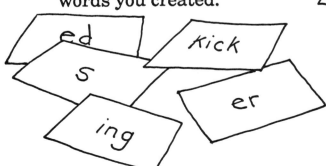

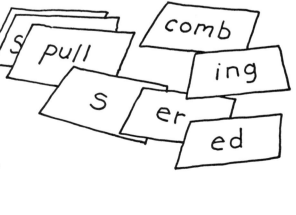

♣ PREFIX PINUP ♣

PURPOSE: Using prefixes

PREPARATION

1. Gather the following materials:
   - wooden clothespins (spring-type)
   - construction paper
   - clothesline
   - felt-tipped pen

2. Print prefixes on clothespins. If plastic ones are used, print prefixes on strips of paper and glue or tape to pins.

3. Make construction paper clothes (see patterns, page 35), and print a root word on each one.

4. String a clothesline across one corner of the classroom or along the chalkboard ledge.

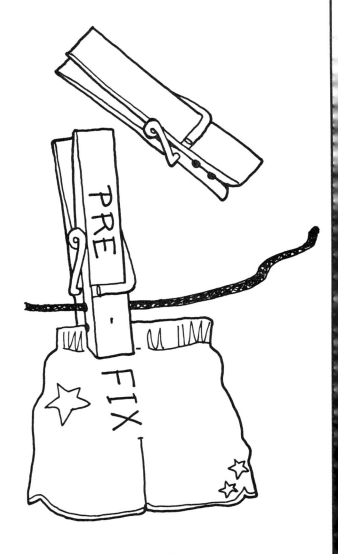

PROCEDURE

Clip the root word clothes to the clothesline using a prefix clothespin that can be combined with the root word to make a new word. Have students take turns reading the new words and discussing their meanings.

WORD SLIDE

The words below are compound words, two words which have been combined to create a new word. Circle one part of each word to "slide" off. Draw a picture to show the entirely different meaning of the remaining word.

1. FISHHOOK
2. NOTEBOOK
3. STRAWBERRY
4. TEAKETTLE
5. SCREWDRIVER
6. CHALKBOARD
7. BUTTERFLY
8. STEPLADDER
9. FOOTBALL
10. COATTAIL
11. INKSTAND

1. _____
2. _____
3. _____
4. _____
5. _____
6. _____
7. _____
8. _____
9. _____
10. _____
11. _____

Name _____ Date _____

COMPOUND CANVAS

Circle all 40 compound words. The words are listed horizontally, vertically, diagonally, forward, and backward.

```
G B R O O M S T I C K N A T I O B D N E R
R C A R D B O A R D A Y L D S T I N N V E
E A A S S A T E D R A Y N R A B D A A E P
E M R N K S T R A W B E R R Y O L L M R A
N P Y O Y E N E Y L E C F R O P O M K Y P
H F A W A B T N P C T I E W R Y E R L O S
O I D M W A A B A R S W E I C A O A I N W
U R H A E L M L A H O R A P L W C F M E E
S E T N V L P C E L I T C E A H S X R G N
E E R N I E G A F F L R H A N G O D O I O
E M I T R E T N I W P L A Y T I M E A B E
R I B I D S U N N A E M I E N H E T D U M
E T F P O S T O R T S P R G U W D B S L O
H E I P A O B T R E C S M N H A A E I O S
T M S N O O E E D R H O A E Y T Y D D N E
O O H O D S K T M F O M N D I E H R E N M
M S E Y U A T A A A O E O V E R C O A T I
D T R D C I O M N L L B A L S M U O U R T
N P M N R I G Y A L Y O E H A E P M P S I
A Y A H O L I A D N A D D O L L H O U S E
R P N A M S E L A S R Y E S U O H D R I B
G R O W N U P P O R D N I A R N H A Y S T
```

Name _____   Date_____

♣ COMPOUND COUNTDOWN ♣

PURPOSE: Recognizing and using compound words

PREPARATION

1. Gather the following materials:
   - clock or timer
   - 5" x 7" index cards
   - felt-tipped pen
   - box
   - paper and pencils

2. Print 20 to 40 words on index cards. Use these or other words:

ball	coat	sail	book	boy	shore	school
brush	place	bone	rain	pan	room	sun
pop	bath	eye	dog	tub	tooth	snow
house	fire	one	man	ship	plane	basket
dish	corn	rail	time	camp	shine	class

3. Place the word cards along with a timer (or clock) and pencils and paper in the box.

PROCEDURE

1. This game is for two players, or may be used as an individual activity.

2. Cards are turned face down in a stack.

3. At the beginning signal, the timer is set, and each player draws a card, reads the word on it, and writes the word on a piece of paper. The player thinks of as many compound words as possible that he or she can make using that word, and lists the compound words under the original word.

4. When the allotted time is over, each player draws another card, writes that word on his or her paper, and continues in the same manner.

5. After fifteen words have been drawn and listed, the player with more compound words on his or her paper wins the game.

COMPOUND MUSEUM

Fill the museum walls with original compound word portraits. The first one is done for you—you do the rest.

List nine more compound words that could be added to the museum collection.

1. _____   2. _____   3. _____

4. _____   5. _____   6. _____

7. _____   8. _____   9. _____

Name _____   Date_____

wear
were

dare
dear

rare
rear

which
witch

their
there

flit
flat

ring
rang

sun
sum

could
cloud

Read the sentence sets below and decide which cloud's word pair goes with each. Write those words in the cloud beside each set. Then complete the sentences by writing in the correct words from the word pair selected.

I'd like to _____ the blue dress.
Where _____ you when I needed you?

This ground is as _____ as my hand.
Fireflies _____ to and fro at dusk.

She ordered her roast beef _____.
That _____ door should be fixed.

The desert _____ is unbelievably hot.
Adding two numbers together will give you the _____.

People go _____ to shop.
_____ dog disappeared.

The Halloween _____ looked scary.
_____ of these bikes do you like best?

I _____ go with you.
The dark _____ moved across the sky.

The telephone bell _____ loudly.
I heard the six o'clock bell _____.

Books are especially _____ to the librarian.
I _____ you to tell that story again.

Name _____ Date _____

©1994 by Incentive Publications, Inc., Nashville, TN.

✤ VOCABULARY VAULT ✤

PURPOSE: Using sight word vocabulary

PREPARATION

1. Gather the
   following materials:
   – oak tag
   – scissors
   – dictionaries
   – colored felt-tipped pens or crayons

2. Direct each student to bring to class an empty shoe box with a top.

3. Cut the oak tag into cards that will fit into the boxes.

4. Distribute a stack of blank cards to each student.

PROCEDURE

1. Students use the colored pens and/or crayons to decorate their boxes, and store the blank cards inside.

2. When a student needs to know the correct spelling or meaning of a word, he or she writes the word on a card and looks it up in the dictionary. The student writes on the card the information found in the dictionary, learns the information, and files the card in the box for future reference.

3. A student may place any word he or she wishes to learn in the box. Words missed on spelling tests and unfamiliar words from content-area texts and reference materials are good additions, too.

4. As the collections grow, students may use their cards as flash cards (two students share cards and check each other), for word games, and in many other settings.

♣ ADD-A-WORD ♣

PURPOSE: Using sight word vocabulary

PREPARATION

1. Gather the following materials:
   - 3" x 5" index cards
   - felt-tipped pen
   - pencils and paper
   - bell

2. Print each of the following and other words of your choice on index cards.

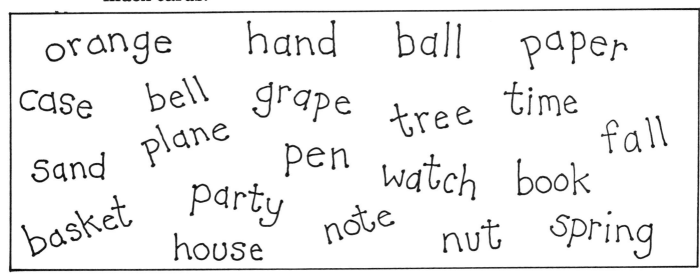

orange   hand   ball   paper
case   bell   grape   tree   time
sand   plane   pen   fall
basket   party   watch   book
house   note   nut   spring

PROCEDURE

1. Players sit in a circle and pass the cards around, each player taking one card from the top of the stack. The cards are not looked at until the bell is rung.

2. At the sound of the bell, cards are turned over. Each player adds one word at a time to the word on the card to give it a new meaning, and repeats this process as many times as possible. No abbreviations or apostrophes are allowed.

3. When the bell sounds again (time limit to be determined before the game begins), cards are passed to the left. Each player then begins a new list with the new word. The game continues in this manner.

4. When "time" is called, lists are compared. A winner is declared for each word, determined by the lengths of the lists.

REBUS RACE

Try your luck at reading these rebuses. Sit where you can see a clock, and time yourself to see how long it takes you to figure out each one. Write each message on the line below its rebus, and record your time in the box.

....

....

....

Name _____ Date_____

Try your luck at reading these rebuses. Sit where you can see a clock, and time yourself to see how long it takes you to figure out each one. Write each message on the line below its rebus, and record your time in the box.

TIME:

....

TIME:

....

TIME:

....

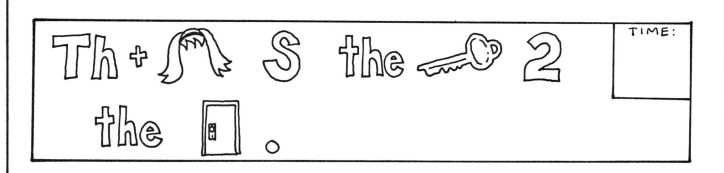

TIME:

....

Name _____ Date_____

♣ IN CONTEXT ♣

PURPOSE: Using context clues

PREPARATION

1. Gather the following materials:
   - 4" x 6" cards
   - file box
   - pencils
   - paper

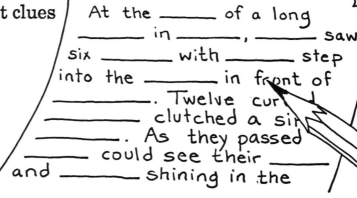

At the _____ of a long _____ in _____, _____ saw six _____ with _____ step into the _____ in front of _____. Twelve cur_ _____ clutched a si_ _____. As they passed _____ could see their _____ and _____ shining in the

2. Make up several one-paragraph stories or take simple short stories from basal texts or classroom newspapers. Eliminate all of the adjectives, nouns, or verbs from each story, and copy them on 4" x 6" index cards, leaving blanks for the omitted words. You may also want to reproduce the stories on page 46 and paste them onto cards to be used as "starters" for your own collection.

3. Place the stories and the Procedure directions in a file box or shoe box.

PROCEDURE

1. Work in pairs to select stories to copy over and fill in the blanks with words of your own choice. Use one card at a time, and then exchange that story with your partner.

2. When your stories are completed, exchange them with each other, and compare and contrast the similarities and differences in your stories.

The cold November wind whistled and moaned as it shook the dead weeds in the fenced garden in front of the empty mansion. Wooden shutters banged noisily against the windows as the wintry wind tried to tear them off their half-broken hinges. The tattered, rotting walls seemed to shake as the icy fists of the storm beat against them. A cold driving rain poured from the cloudy, forbidding sky, turning the deserted garden into a sullen black lake that slowly and menacingly crept up to the crumbling concrete steps. The dead leaves floated like ghostly ships in the rising waters. A yellow flashing streak of lightning appeared in the sky and hit an old dead oak tree beside the house. The stricken tree quivered and rocked back and forth on its rotten roots. Slowly and silently, it began to fall.

On a sunny spring morning, the huge giant walked softly through his lovely garden. Suddenly, he saw a golden bird sitting on the lowest limb of a blooming tree. The bird was singing a sweet song that reminded the giant of his youth. He ran toward the bird with nothing but kindness in his heart, but the gentle bird was frightened and flew into the sky. The giant stopped on the path and called to the bird to return, but the bird had flown far away.

GRAMMAR CRACKER CAKE

Nouns and verbs and other parts of speech are recipe ingredients for sentences. They must be combined correctly so that a sentence will present a whole thought.

Read the recipe directions below. Tell the part of speech of each underlined word by writing its name in the crossword puzzle.

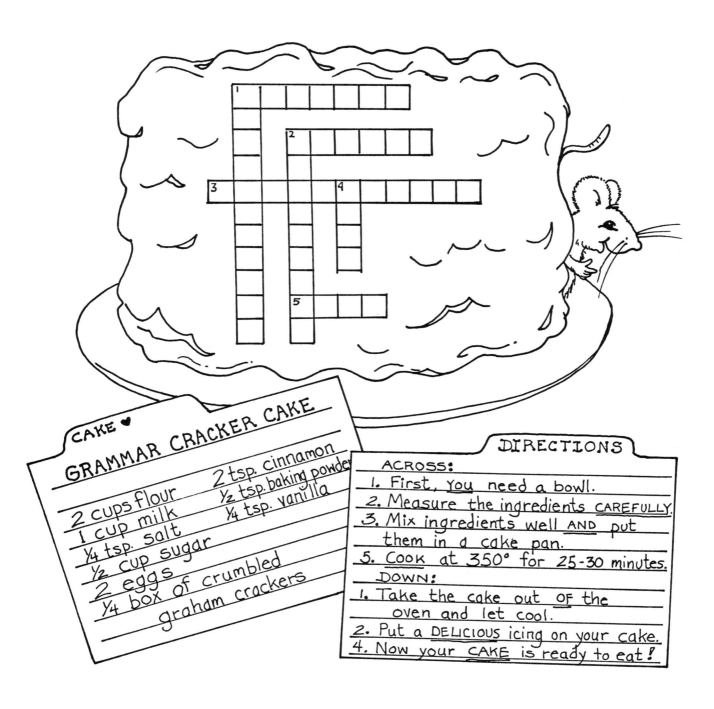

GRAMMAR CRACKER CAKE

CAKE ♥

2 cups flour
1 cup milk
¼ tsp. salt
½ cup sugar
2 eggs
¼ box of crumbled graham crackers

2 tsp. cinnamon
½ tsp. baking powder
¼ tsp. vanilla

DIRECTIONS

ACROSS:
1. First, <u>you</u> need a bowl.
2. Measure the ingredients <u>CAREFULLY</u>.
3. Mix ingredients well <u>AND</u> put them in a cake pan.
5. Cook at 350° for 25-30 minutes.
DOWN:
1. Take the cake out <u>OF</u> the oven and let cool.
2. Put a <u>DELICIOUS</u> icing on your cake.
4. Now your <u>CAKE</u> is ready to eat!

Name _____ Date_____

CLASSIFICATION JUMBLE

All of these packages came tumbling into the Classification Center. Please help restore order by drawing a line through the word in each package that does not belong and writing a classification word for the remaining words on the line below each package. (Use your dictionary if you need help.)

Write 3 words for each classification word listed on the boxes at the bottom of the page.

Example:

yacht
canoe
~~airplane~~
tug

boats

1
parka
jacket
muffler
shorts

2
poultry
pastry
parrot
pasta

THIS END UP

4
encyclopedia
chalk
dictionary
atlas

5
castle
cabin
poncho
mansion

3
weasel
lily
angora
aardvark

6
kale
zucchini
apple
broccoli

8
New York City
Canada
England
Mexico

7
humid
freezing
sunny
growing

9
bucket pint
gallon quart

Plants

Oceans

Fruits

Name _____   Date_____

✤ ON THE FLIP SIDE ✤

PURPOSE: Understanding multiple meanings

PREPARATION

1. Cut record or compact disc shapes from black construction paper.

2. Use white chalk or crayon to print on each disc a word that has several meanings.
   Examples: trunk   light
                   run   up
                   back   turn
                   set   order

3. Provide white chalk or crayons and the Procedure directions for student use.

PROCEDURE

1. Draw pictures to show different meanings of the word on the disc.

2. "Flip" the disc, and write one sentence using each meaning of the word.

"Seymour the elephant used his trunk to load his clothes trunk into the trunk of the car."

♣ PAIR UP ♣

PURPOSE: Using homonyms

PREPARATION

1. Gather the following materials:
   - game cards
   - scissors
   - red pen
   - green pen

2. Cut out the words on the Pair Up worksheet (page 51) to make nine sets of homonym cards and an illustration for one word in each of the sets (only one word is illustrated, not both).

3. Make a red X on one word in each pair and a green X on the other.

4. Make three stacks of cards—one with red X's, one with green X's, and one with illustrations.

PROCEDURE

1. This game is for two players.

2. The three stacks of cards are placed in the middle of the table.

3. Divide one stack of word cards equally between the two players. The other two stacks remain in the center of the table.

4. The first player draws a card from the word card stack. If this card contains a homonym for a card in his or her hand, the player places the pair on the table in front of him or her and draws another card. If not, he or she may keep that card, and must add one card from his or her hand to the bottom of the word stack on the table.

5. The next player takes a turn and repeats the same procedure.

6. Each time a player gets a homonym pair, he or she may draw a card from the stack of illustrations. If the illustration matches any pair the player has on the table, he or she may keep it and add it to the pair. If not, he or she may add it to his or her hand, and add another card to the bottom of the stack from his or her hand (either word or illustration stack, depending on which is discarded).

7. The first person to make five pairs or to get two pairs with matching illustrations wins the game.

stare	stair	
scent	cent	
pair	pear	
plane	plain	
flower	flour	
waist	waste	
root	route	
steak	stake	
fowl	foul	

✤ THE LEANING TOWER OF PAIRS ✤

PURPOSE: Using synonyms, antonyms, and homonyms

PREPARATION

1. Enlarge and reproduce the "Leaning Tower of Pairs" game board (page 53). Glue it into a file folder, or put it on tagboard.

2. Cut out 120-140 tagboard squares to make 60-70 pairs of synonym, antonym, and homonym cards. Write the words on the cards.

3. Place the cards in the folder, and make the game available for individual student use. Provide a clock or timer for the game.

4. Write the following directions on the front of the folder.

PROCEDURE

1. This game is a race against the clock. Set the timer for the specified time, and begin.

2. Turn 20 cards face up on the table.

3. Find a synonym, antonym, or homonym pair, and place these two cards on the tower, beginning at the bottom left corner and working from left to right. Continue to do this with all the pairs you can make with the first 20 cards.

4. Drawing one more card at a time, pair all the cards and place them in the tower. Try to fill the entire tower before your time runs out.

5. When your time has expired, count the pairs you have placed in the tower. On the back of the folder, record your name, the number of pairs placed, and how much time you used. Challenge a classmate to beat your time.

✤ VOCABULARY VARIETY ✤

PURPOSE: Using content-area vocabulary

PREPARATION

1. Gather the following materials:
   - five flat boxes (hosiery or handkerchief boxes are fine)
   - felt-tipped pens
   - construction paper in 5 colors
   - 3″ x 5″ index cards

2. Cover the boxes with construction paper and decorate to look like books. Use felt-tipped pens to write these words as titles on the "books":
   - Social Studies
   - Math
   - Science
   - Music
   - Art

3. On the cards, print words associated with each of these content areas appropriate to the grade level of the students. To make this activity self-checking, place dots on the backs of the cards corresponding to the different colors of construction paper on each box.

Examples:

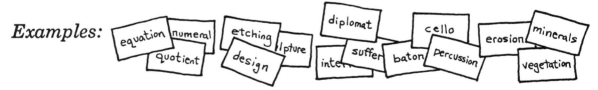

4. Place the boxes and all the word cards in a learning center, or assign as an independent activity.

PROCEDURE

Sort cards and place them in the appropriate boxes.

GREETINGS

The nicest greeting cards are ones that are made by hand for a special person.

Match words and phrases from the two columns below to make messages to send for each of the occasions listed. Write each message on the line next to the appropriate occasion.

Sending . . .	. . . concern
May this be . . .	. . . happy thoughts
Please accept . . .	. . . the best one yet
Sincere . . .	. . . special wishes
Thinking . . .	. . . congratulations
Offering . . .	. . . you well
Wishing . . .	. . . my appreciation

BIRTHDAY ·_____

THANKYOU ·_____

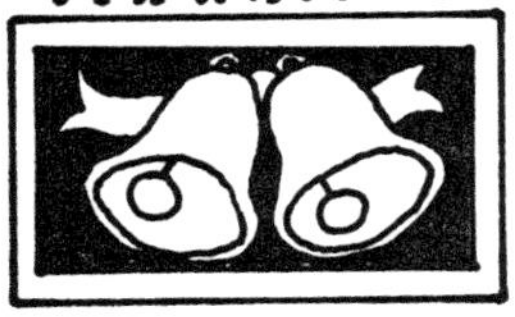

ANNIVERSARY ·_____

ILLNESS ·_____

HOLIDAY ·_____

FRIENDSHIPS ·_____

SYMPATHY ·_____

Design a special occasion card for a friend, and write your own message in five words or less.

Name _____   Date_____

✤ AN ORANGE IS AN ORANGE ✤

PURPOSE: Forming sensory impressions

PREPARATION

1. Provide an orange, paper, pencils, and crayons for each student.

2. Give the following directions to the students.

PROCEDURE

1. Take two minutes to look at, feel, smell, and study your orange.

2. List at least 10 words that describe the orange.

3. Write the names of three food dishes that may be made with oranges or orange juice.

4. Make up an original recipe using oranges. Write the recipe on a sheet of paper, and illustrate it in color.

Sweet, bumpy, fresh, tempting, tender, juicy, tangy...

OR

Describe a new and creative way to use oranges. Draw and color a picture to illustrate the use.

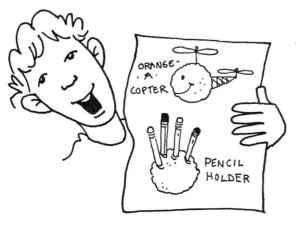

ORANGE-A-COPTER

PENCIL HOLDER

5. After you complete your work, your next job is to eat your orange!

✤ SENSATIONAL SENTENCES ✤

PURPOSE: Interpreting and conveying moods created by words

PREPARATION

1. Reproduce copies of the Sensational Sentences worksheet (page 58) for the students.

2. Write the Procedure directions on the chalkboard.

PROCEDURE

1. Combine one word or phrase from each of the three columns to make as many sentences as possible. Words and phrases may be used more than once, as long as they are not used twice in the same sentence combination.

2. Check to make sure your sentences are complete and correct.

3. Select five of your sentences to illustrate on the back of the Sensational Sentences worksheet.

In the distance... a dog howled.... wearily.

SENSATIONAL SENTENCES

I	II	III
Sparkled with sunshine	The unicorn is	Gregariously
Most of the time	My teacher smiled	Triumphant
Before dawn	The king marched	A sinking feeling
At half past eight	Winners are	Classically elegant
On the bright side	A dog howled	Guilty
Yesterday	My sister looked	Fiercely proud
As the whistle blew	Kittens purr	Desperately lonely
Every now and then	The patient reported	Lively and alert
After dinner	Film stars appear	Contentedly
In the distance	A baby clapped	Joyfully
From day to day	Grandmother rocked	Wearily

Sentences

1. _____

2. _____

3. _____

4. _____

5. _____

6. _____

7. _____

8. _____

9. _____

10. _____

11. _____

Most of the time... Kittens purr... contentedly.

Yesterday... my teacher smiled... joyfully!

Every now and then... the baby clapped.... triumphant!

Name _____ Date _____

✤ HUE ME IN! ✤

PURPOSE: Interpreting and conveying moods created by words

PREPARATION

1. Write a different descriptive phrase or sentence conveying an "environmental" mood on sheets of drawing paper (one sheet for each student).

    Examples to use:

    The rutted, rocky road led through the tall, menacing mountains which were covered with huge trees and overgrown shrubs.

    . . . dusty, dark trail through the deep forest . . .

    . . . midnight, the mysterious and malevolent witching hour . . .

    An eerie stillness spread over the city sidewalks . . .

    The bright sunshine seemed to illuminate the vivid sky and bring a touch of sheer magic to the desert sunset.

2. Fold the sheets, and distribute one to each student as you read aloud the Procedure directions.

PROCEDURE

1. Each student reads his or her descriptive passage and selects only one crayon to use to illustrate it.

2. The object is to use the crayon in varying levels of intensity and shading to convey the mood and feel of the passage.

3. Sharing and discussing the impressions and completed illustrations are important aspects of this activity.

Have you checked your holiday vocabulary lately? Here's a little test to help you do just that.

1. Fill in the missing vowels in the words.
2. Draw a line from the name of each holiday to the symbol that is associated with it.
3. Draw a line to another word associated with the same holiday. (Use your dictionary for help if you need it.)

One holiday is done for you. You do the rest.

mistletoe

r_bb_t

L_pr_ch__n

Christmas

Ch_n_k_h

r_s_l_t__ns

V_l_nt_n_s D_y

l_v_

P_ss_v_r

St. P_tr_ck's D_y

Th_nksg_v_ng

Native Ame_i_an

E_st_r

m_tz_s

w_tch

l_tk_

N_w Y__r's D_y

H_ll_w__n

Name _____ Date_____

♣ ON THE WORD TRACK ♣

PURPOSE: Recognizing word relationships

PREPARATION

1. Print one of the category words below (or substitute your own) on each railroad car on the worksheet on page 62. Then reproduce a copy of the worksheet for each student.

Categories

mood	weight	careers	holidays
size	color	animals	weather
age	time	plants	transportation

2. Provide dictionaries and a thesaurus for student use.

3. Place in a learning center setting, or use as seat work or homework.

ON THE WORD TRACK

Fill each railroad car with words related to the category word. If you think of more words than you can fit into the space, write the category word on the back of your paper, and list the rest of your words under it.

Name _____   Date_____

CONSTRUCTION CREW

All newspaper reporters know that every news article should include information on who, when, where, why, and what happened. The best reporters hold their reader's attention by adding enough descriptive words or phrases to give the writing "pizzazz."

Each of these sentences tells something that happened to someone. In other words, you have the "who" and the "what." Add one word or phrase from each column below to make these simple, unexciting sentences more interesting. Use each word or phrase only once.

WHERE	WHEN	"PIZZAZZ"
on another planet	last Sunday	bewitching
at the beach	on the stroke of 12	gorgeous
on a city street	just before dark	magnificent
at the cave's entrance	a year ago today	hideous
in the garden	yesterday	unrealistic
at the museum	week before last	glamorous
over the rainbow	at dawn	heartbreaking

1. She bought the blouse.

   over the rainbow

2. We saw the sunset.

   on another planet

3. I lost my kite.

   at the beach

4. He heard that screech.

   on the stroke of 12

5. Mother smelled a rose.

   at the museum

6. The girl's tears fell.

   on another planet

7. She heard the news.

   a year ago today

Name _Rhapsody_   Date _05/01/25_

❖ WORD OF THE DAY ❖

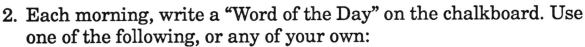

PURPOSE: Word appreciation

PREPARATION

1. You will need the following materials:
   – chalkboard
   – pencils
   – paper

2. Each morning, write a "Word of the Day" on the chalkboard. Use one of the following, or any of your own:

light	snow	boat	coat
rain	school	sun	night
day	house	fire	life

PROCEDURE

1. During the day, students make lists of as many words as they can that contain the "Word of the Day." Hyphenated or compound words may be used.
   Examples: raincoat — raindrop — rainbow — rain hat
   At the end of the day, compare lists to see who has the most words.

2. Or students write as many words as they can that have the same ending sound as the "Word of the Day."

3. Or students write a story using the "Word of the Day" as many times as possible.

4. Or students try to find the word in everything read all day long (texts and library books, newspapers, classroom charts, etc.) and make a list of the number of times the word is found, giving the sources and page numbers.

Write a story about Vicki and Victor's visit to Vacation Village. Use as many words beginning with the letter "V" in the story as you can.

_____

_____

_____

_____

_____

_____

_____

_____

_____

_____

Word List (Use your dictionary to find more.)

villa	vague	vagabond	vegetable	very
vacancy	villager	vehicle	vice	vinegar
voyage	valid	visitor	vain	vanguard

Name _____ Date_____

©1994 by Incentive Publications, Inc., Nashville, TN.

❖ TOPIC CENTERED ❖

PURPOSE: Categorization/word association

PREPARATION

1. Write topics well known to students on sheets of drawing paper or newsprint. Provide a sheet for each student.

2. Fold the papers in half, and place in a basket.

PROCEDURE

1. Pass the basket, and allow each student to remove a folded sheet of paper.

2. Using a pencil and/or crayons, the students write as many words pertaining to the topic as possible in a specified time. Dictionaries may be used if necessary.

3. The student with the most words correctly spelled at the end of the specified time wins the game.

4. Allow time for the completed sheets to be illustrated.

ADAPTATION

If a particular unit is being studied, all students may use the same unit-related topic. They might be asked to try for at least one word beginning with each letter of the alphabet, or for all three-syllable (or more) words, or the topic may be written on the chalkboard so that students may add words throughout the day.

APPLE TREATS

Think about the many different ways we use apples. Add one extra word to each apple in the basket to make an apple treat. If you think of more ways to use apples than there are apples in the basket, write in some extra ones on the blank recipe card!

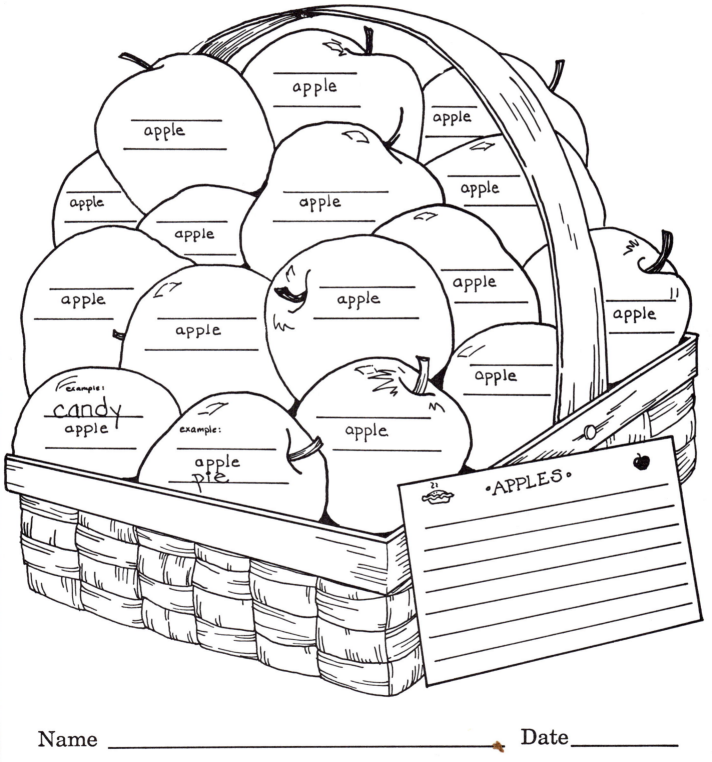

Name _____   Date _____

CINDERELLA'S CLOSET

Cinderella's closet is a mess! She's been kept so busy scrubbing floors and doing errands for her mean stepsisters that she has had little time for herself.

Help her get ready to leave with the prince by marking out the item in each box that does not belong.

Name _____ Date _____

✤ LOGICAL LINE-UP ✤

PURPOSE: Listing ideas in proper sequence

PREPARATION

1. Cut out stories or articles from classroom newspapers or magazines. Then cut the articles into sentence strips.

2. Place the sentence strips in envelopes, and label each with the title or main idea of the material.

3. Place the envelopes in a learning center or free-work area, and provide paper, pencils, and the following directions. (If working with children who need extra reinforcement, you may need to provide the uncut newspaper or magazine article for checking purposes.)

PROCEDURE

1. Read all the sentence strips carefully.

2. Select the main idea of the story or article first. Then order the sentences as you think they occurred originally in the article.

3. Write a one-paragraph summary of the story or article. Be sure to include all of the important ideas in the order in which they occurred in the original story or article.

4. Compare your summary with one written by a classmate.

✿ SEQUENCE OF EVENTS ✿

PURPOSE: Sequencing

PREPARATION

1. Gather the following materials:
   - envelopes
   - comic strips
   - pencils and paper
   - box with top

2. Collect one-strip comics, or draw your own (with or without words).

3. Cut the strips apart, and place in an envelope. Prepare at least six or eight envelopes for variety.

4. Place all the envelopes in a box, and add pencils and paper. Print the following directions inside the top of the box.

PROCEDURE

1. Take one envelope at a time from the box. Place all the frames from the comic strip before you, and look carefully at each one.

2. Arrange the frames in sequence to tell the story.

3. After you have done several, select one you like and draw another strip with exactly the same number of frames. Show what you think might happen next.

PURPOSE: Drawing conclusions

PREPARATION

1. Gather the following materials:
   - game board
   - 24 3" x 5" index cards
   - timer
   - felt-tipped pen

2. Enlarge the Think Tank game board (page 72).

3. Prepare two sets of cards, 12 to each set. Make six pairs of cards per set by writing a "Think Tank" sentence on one card per pair and a logical conclusion for that sentence on the other. Mark each pair of cards with numbers, dots, or any other symbols to make this activity self-checking. Use these sentences for starters, if you like.

4. Place the game board in a free-time area in the classroom, and arrange the "Think Tank" cards face up around the board. Stack the conclusion cards inside the "Tank" in the center of the board.

PROCEDURE

1. Two players take turns drawing one card at a time and trying to match it with the proper "Think Tank" card on the board. The timer should be used, and if the card is not matched in a specified time, the player must put the card drawn on the bottom of the stack and forfeit that turn. If the card can be matched in the given time, the player picks up the "Think Tank" card and keeps the pair.

2. The game continues until all cards have been paired. The player with more pairs wins the game.

CONCLUDING CONCLUSIONS

Finish the following diagrams by "reading" them and drawing picture conclusions in the spaces provided.

Name _____ Date _____

JUST BECAUSE

The pictures in eight of these circles show something that happened. Each picture in the other eight circles shows an effect of one of the happenings. Draw lines to connect each "cause" circle with its correct "effect" circle.

Select one cause and effect circle set to use as the theme for a creative story.

Name _____ Date_____

✤ WITH PEN IN HAND ✤

PURPOSE: Sensitivity to author's purpose

PREPARATION

1. Provide dual copies of paperback books, or reproduce two copies of a story or an excerpt so that two students have the identical material. Selections should be based on a well-developed character portrait of two or more interacting characters, like those found in the following:

   Sleeping Beauty — Sleeping Beauty and the Good Fairy

   Hansel and Gretel — Gretel and the Stepmother

   Cinderella — Cinderella and the oldest stepsister

   The Adventures of Robin Hood — Robin Hood and Maid Marian

   Winnie the Pooh — Piglet and Pooh

   Little Women — Jo and Beth

   Madeline — Madeline and Miss Clavel

PROCEDURE

1. Working in pairs, students read the selected material. Then each chooses to represent one of the two main characters.

2. Each student writes a letter as if from the story character he or she represents to the other story character, expressing a personal view of some particular topic or event in the story with implications for the other and/or for common acquaintances.

3. Letters are put in envelopes, addressed, and exchanged. Without any discussion between the students, the letters are read and answered.

4. After the response letters are exchanged and read, the two students verbally share the viewpoints expressed and discuss any conflicts of opinion or perception caused by each character's position.

✣ PLOT A CHARACTERIZATION ✣

PURPOSE: Identifying character traits

PREPARATION

1. Reproduce the Plot A Characterization worksheet (page 77).

2. Guide each student in selecting a book that portrays one person's life. Biographies and autobiographies are natural choices, but other selections may be appropriate for special student needs. Fiction may be of more interest in some situations.

PROCEDURE

1. Follow the directions on the Plot a Characterization worksheet.

2. Display copies of completed worksheets for discussion.

PLOT A CHARACTERIZATION

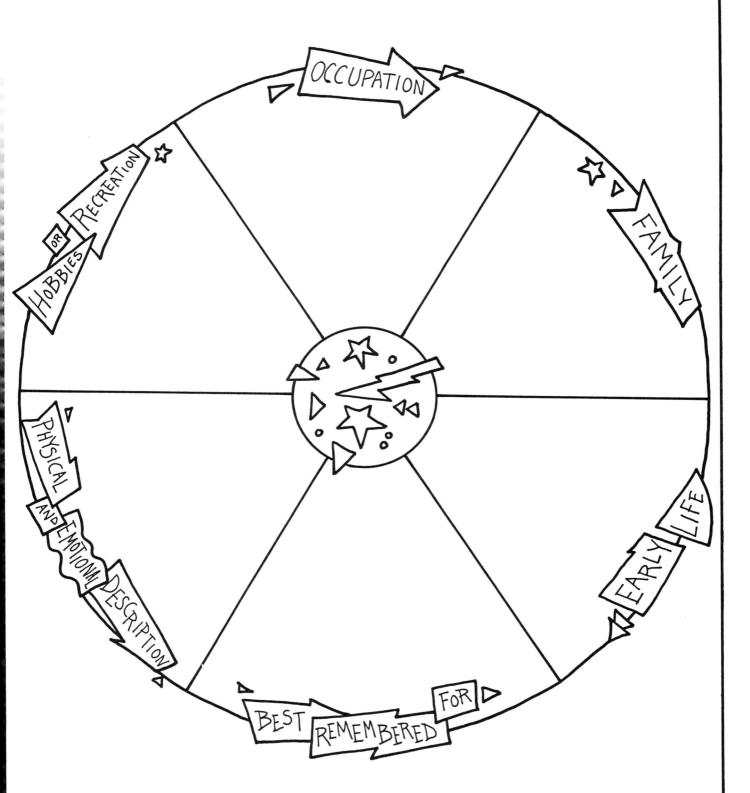

Write events, words, phrases, descriptive sentences or other information about the person being characterized in each spoke of the wheel. Then fill the center circle with words that describe the person's character.

Name _____ Date_____

♣ FINGER TALK ♣

Select any three to six puppets from page 79 to be characters in a play. Color and cut out the puppets, and tape the rings together to fit your fingers. Write the dialog for a play in which the puppets you have chosen will "act." Give your players very strong character traits to make the play more interesting. Practice your play, and present it to the class.

✤ STORIES TO BUILD ✤

PURPOSE: Sensitivity to plot and sequence

PREPARATION

1. Reproduce the story beginnings on page 81. Cut the sentences apart, and place them in large envelopes.

2. Add paper and pencils for student use.

3. Make the complete story beginnings available to students for self-checking.

4. Write the following directions on the front of each envelope.

PROCEDURE

1. Take all of the sentences out of the envelope and spread them out in front of you.

2. Read each one carefully. Then build the story by arranging the sentences in the correct sequence.

3. After you have arranged the sentences to begin the story, use the paper and pencil to write an ending for the story. Remember to build plot and sequence, and make your ending as exciting as possible.

4. Sign your name as author and put it in the envelope for others to read.

STORIES TO BUILD

An Underground Adventure

Tom and Jerry are good friends.

They play together almost every day.

Three of their favorite games are "wood tag," "kick the can," and "I spy."

One day, they were playing in a vacant lot when they saw a big hole in the ground.

As they looked more closely at the hole, they discovered that it was actually the opening to a big underground tunnel.

Naturally, they decided to crawl into the hole and do a bit of underground exploring.

Tom crawled in slowly, and Jerry was right behind him.

A Trip To The Zoo

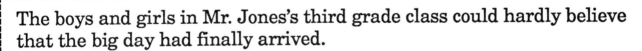

The boys and girls in Mr. Jones's third grade class could hardly believe that the big day had finally arrived.

For weeks, they had been preparing for their trip to the zoo.

As they climbed into the big, yellow bus for the fifteen-mile ride, they were filled with excitement and expectations.

The bus driver discussed rules, and Mr. Jones gave each student a map and a booklet about the animals in the zoo.

Just as the driver called, "Let's go," and started the motor, Mrs. Goodlady, the principal, came to the door of the school and yelled, "Stop! Stop where you are!"

✤ CARTOON CREATIONS ✤

PURPOSE: Visualizing

PREPARATION

1. Cut topics from newspapers or magazines, or write titles appropriate for "cartoon creations" on strips of paper.

2. Place the captions in a basket with a handle or in a plastic pail. Add paper and felt-tipped pens.

3. Write "Cartoon Creations" on the cover of a loose leaf notebook. Place the basket or pail and the "Cartoon Creations" notebook in a free-choice interest center. Print the following directions on a study guide and add to the center.

PROCEDURE

1. Select a cartoon creation.

2. Use a sheet of paper and pens from the basket to illustrate the caption.

3. Sign your cartoon, and add it to the "Cartoon Creations" notebook.

✤ LETTERED LUNCHES ✤

The children at Andover school are having trouble finding their own lunch boxes. Help them by cutting out the lunch boxes below and pasting each one in its alphabetically assigned space on the lettered lunch shelves.

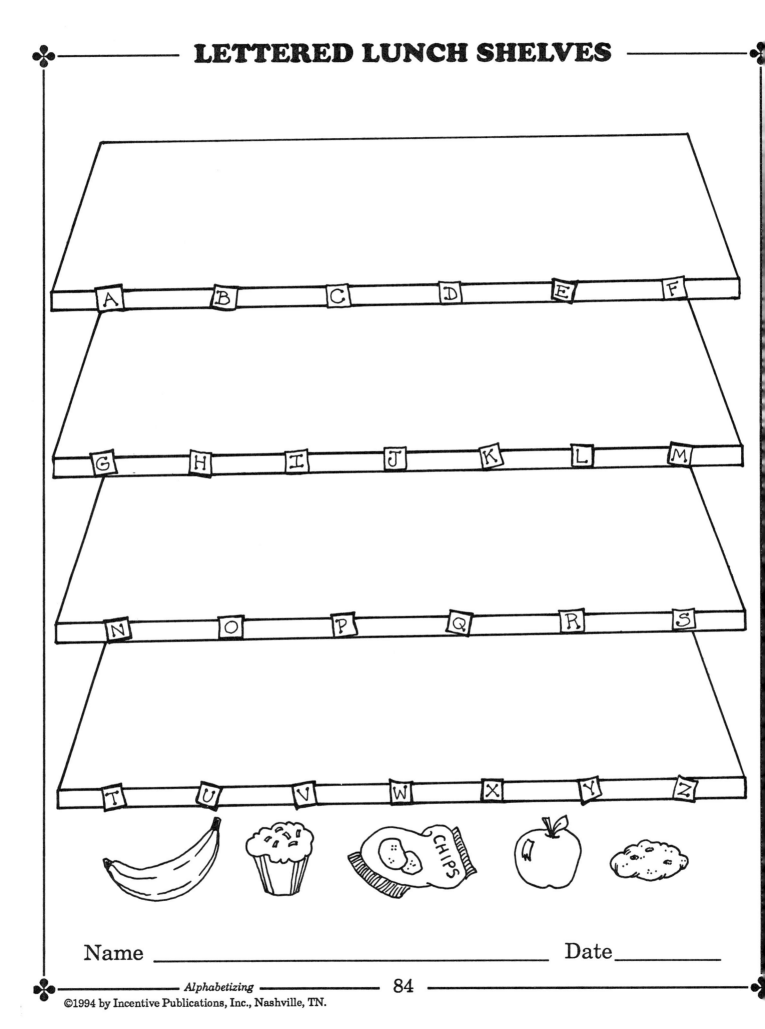

Name _____   Date_____

✤ OOPS! WRONG PAGE! ✤

Cross out the words that do not belong on each dictionary page. Use the guide words to help you decide which words don't fit in.

cow — **cut**

come   cub
crab   chair
creek   curl
crow   curly
crown   cut

leg — **live**

lemon   limp
let   lap
lie   line
light   list
laugh   love

men — **mouse**

mess   miss
milk   mix
mad   meat
mat   mop
mile   mother

pat — **puppy**

paw   pizza
pen   plane
pet   dog
pick   play
bat   pool

seal — **soon**

see   sick
set   sat
shark   sister
chip   sleep
ship   snake

hello — **hurry**

hen   hog
hide   hop
he   hot
hill   hug
hat   hurt

❖ CONTEMPLATING THE CONTENTS ❖

PURPOSE: Using a table of contents

PREPARATION

1. Choose a book of common interest to students that contains a table of contents (example: *The Wind in the Willows).*

2. Go through the book, and choose one word from each consecutive chapter to put together to make a message for the students. Be sure that the words you have chosen will fit together in the order the students find them to form a sensible sentence.

Chart Format

Chapter Title	Page #	Para-graph #	Sen-tence #	Word #	Word
	1	1	1	2	
	23	2	3	15	
	43	1	3	11	
	67	1	1	43	
	82	1	2	28	
	109	1	4	15	
	135	2	3	117	

3. Make a chart like the one above using the book of your choice. Leave the "Chapter Title" and "Word" columns blank.

4. Place the book, the chart, some paper and pencils, and the following directions in a free-choice activity center for individual student use.

PROCEDURE

1. Divide your paper into two columns.

2. In the first column, fill in each chapter title in the order in which it appears in the book.

CONTEMPLATING THE CONTENTS

3. Follow the directions on the chart to find the words in the message. Fill in each word from a chapter beside the chapter title. *(Note to the teacher: You may want to complete the first line for your students.)*

4. Write your completed sentence across the bottom of the page.

5. Illustrate your paper with characters and scenes from the book.

Sample Chart using *The Wind in the Willows*

Chapter Title	Page #	Paragraph #	Sentence #	Word #	Word
The River Bank	1	1	1	2	MOLE
The Open Road	23	2	3	15	AND
The Wild	43	1	3	11	RAT
Mr. Badger	67	1	1	43	HAVE
Dulce Domum	82	1	2	28	HAD
Mr. Toad	109	1	4	15	SOME
The Piper at the Gates of Dawn	135	2	3	117	SPLENDID
Toad's Adventures	145	2	1	6	HOURS
Wayfarers All	165	2	2	41	ON
The further Adventures of Toad	189	1	1	1	THE
Like summer Tempests came His Tears	216	2	6	19	RIVER
The Return of Ulysses	240	3	2	27	BANK

Completed Sentence: <u>Mole and Rat have had</u>
<u>Some splendid hours on the river bank.</u>

Name _____ Date_____

A PLAIN PAPER PLANE PLAN

Follow this diagram to make a paper airplane.

1.

2.

3.

4.

5.

6.

7.

8.

9.

When you have finished, decorate your airplane. Then at recess, have a paper plane race.

Name _____ Date _____

❖ PUNCTUATION POINTERS ❖

Point out what you know! Work the crossword puzzle to show your knowledge of punctuation skills.

Across

2. When a sentence asks something, a _____ mark goes at the end of it.

3. Use a _____ to separate words in a series.

5. A sentence that shows excitement ends with a (an) _____ mark.

6. Every _____ must have a verb and a subject.

Down

1. A _____ comes at the end of a telling sentence.

2. When you write something down just exactly as someone said it, you put _____ marks around what was said.

4. What comes at the end of an abbreviation like "Mr___"?

Decide which color each punctuation mark makes you think of, and color in the marks. Display your finished page.

Name _____ Date_____

❖ LITTLE BOOKS TELL A LOT ❖

PURPOSE: Reading and following written directions

PREPARATION

1. Reproduce the Little Books Tell A Lot worksheet (page 91).

2. Gather pencils, paper, crayons and/or felt-tipped pens for the students.

PROCEDURE

1. Distribute the worksheets.

2. Discuss the assignment with the students, but do not demonstrate how to make the book. (A completed book might be shown to those students needing more guidance.)

FOLLOW-UP ACTIVITY

Ask students to select a "Little Book" to review. Arrange a time for book reviews to be presented to the entire group.

LITTLE BOOKS TELL A LOT

1. Horizontally fold a sheet of 8½" x 11" white paper down the middle.

2. Vertically fold the folded sheet to make 4 "pages."

3. Use the scissors to clip through the first fold (almost but not quite all the way across), leaving the paper joined at the center point.

4. Now, you should have a tiny book with 8 pages (counting fronts and backs). Number the pages in the upper left hand corners.

5. Select one of the following titles, and write a book about it.

6. Design an attractive cover for the book on page 1. Don't forget to write your own name as author.

7. Write a copyright notice on the inside front cover (page 2). (Use a library book for reference if you need it.)

8. On page 3, which is actually the title page of your book, write the title and your name again. Illustrate this page.

9. Plan pages 4, 5, 6, and 7 carefully to tell your entire story. Make it complete and interesting to hold the reader's attention.

10. Design a back cover for page 8.

11. Place your completed book on the reading table to share with your classmates.

Follow these directions to complete the "Fruit Salad" poster. You will need a pencil and some crayons.

1. Write your name under the basket.
2. Draw another leaf on the stem of the apple.
3. Color the apple red, and the stem and leaves green.
4. Write the names of three fruits besides pear that begin with the letter "p."
5. Give the pear a smiling face.
6. Use your pencil to add enough grapes to make an even dozen.
7. Write four words on the banana describing how it would taste.
8. Draw a handle on the basket.
9. Use your favorite crayon to draw a big bow on the handle.
10. Color all of the fruits.
11. Write a recipe for fruit salad on the back of the sheet.

Name _____ Date_____

The Great Consonant Case, page 11

If you work carefully, you can find the missing consonants right under Sly Sam the Sleuth's eyes. Circle a consonant when you put it in its proper place, and you will know not to go looking for it again.

Sly Sam has been assigned to the Great Consonant Case. Consonants keep disappearing in large numbers right out of otherwise sensible sentences. More consonants are missing every day. The words are beginning to panic, and though Sly Sam is smart and brave, even he is desperate. Can you come to his rescue?

Please hurry and replace the missing consonants to return peace and quiet to Sly Sam's world.

Message: "Thanks !!"

Is It "D" or "T"?, page 14

D				T	
Charged	Dreamed	Added		Looked	Tracked
Allowed	Tamed	Salted		Smoked	Bricked
Called	Thrilled	Entered		Shocked	Thanked
Rolled	Framed			Walked	Picked
Planted	Filled			Bumped	Jerked
Followed	Harmed			Stacked	Tricked
				Marched	Dumped
				Slashed	

Letter-ing, page 15

Doubled Letter-ing			Dropped Letter-ing		
Hopping	Planning	Fanning	Timing	Snoring	Loving
Sitting	Swimming	Trimming	Coming	Striking	Hoping
Batting	Grinning	Tapping	Waking	Living	Liking

Compound Canvas, page 37

Broomstick	Strawberry	Everyone	Grownup
Cardboard	Someone	Chairman	Sunflower
Greenhouse	Milkman	Watermelon	Farmland
Playtime	Highway	Someday	Postman
Grandmother	Baseball	Bedroom	Basketball
Campfire	Fisherman	Roadside	Nobody
Sometime	Snowman	Birdhouse	Airplane
Driveway	Waterfall	Salesman	Dollhouse
Playmate	Schoolyard	Barnyard	Overcoat
Cannot	Somebody	Firewood	Birthday